Why the critics loved

Elegant and Easy Rooms

"Author Dylan La... ...oose paint from
a paint chip, how ...u should spend
on a rug, why ob ...nd on. Tightly
written and filled ...read for do-it-
yourself design m

—*Newsday*

"If the choicest th ...e wrecking ball
just yet. Instead, ...living space a
face-lift."

—*Cosmopolitan*

"The secrets are ...indow, how to
heighten a room ...st a few of the
myriad topics tha

Victorian Homes

"Truly helpful hin

Washington Post

"What it promises ...an inside track
to the best profe: ...s to the art of
display."

...*rating Magazine*

Books by Dylan Landis

Metropolitan Home: American Style
Elegant and Easy Rooms
Elegant and Easy Foyers, Halls, and Stairs
Elegant and Easy Living Rooms
Designing for Small Homes
Checklist for Your New Baby
Your Healthy Pregnancy Workbook
Your Healthy Child's Medical Workbook
Your Health & Medical Workbook

Elegant and Easy
Bedrooms

100 Trade Secrets for Designing with Style

DYLAN LANDIS

Drawings by David McGrievey

A DELL TRADE PAPERBACK

A DELL TRADE PAPERBACK
Published by
Dell Publishing
a division of
Random House, Inc.
1540 Broadway
New York, New York 10036

Dell books may be purchased for business or promotional use or for special sales. For information please write to: Special Markets Department, Random House, Inc., 1540 Broadway, New York, NY 10036.

DTP and the colophon are trademarks of Random House, Inc.

Library of Congress Cataloging-in-Publication
Landis, Dylan, 1956–
Elegant and easy bedrooms: 100 trade secrets for designing with style / Dylan Landis; drawings by David McGrievey.
p. cm.
ISBN 0-440-50861-4
1. Bedrooms. 2. Interior decoration. I. Title.
NK2117.B33 L35 2000
747.7'7—dc21
99-045352

Printed in the United States of America

Published simultaneously in Canada

April 2000

10 9 8 7 6 5 4 3 2 1

FFG

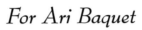

For Ari Baquet

ACKNOWLEDGMENTS

The best part of writing the Elegant and Easy books was discovering, again and again, how generous designers can be with their hard-won trade secrets. Those named on these pages were also generous with their time, making it a challenge to single anyone out—but I am particularly grateful to Kim DePole, Christopher Fox, and Barbara Southerland for providing an abundance of ideas, and to Barry Goralnick, architect and friend, who taught me much about good design.

Kenneth X. Charbonneau of Benjamin Moore shared his expertise on color. Neil Janovic of Janovic/Plaza Decorating Centers fielded my questions about paint. Erica Landis and Dean Baquet, both passionate about decorating, improved the manuscript with their thorough readings. And David McGrievey gave the book charm and spirit through his drawings.

My warmest thanks, as always, go to my literary agent, Dominick Abel. And I am fortunate to have worked with two terrific editors at Dell—Mary Ellen O'Neill, who launched the Elegant and Easy series, and Kathleen Jayes, who wrapped it up.

CONTENTS

Elegant and Easy Bedrooms

100 Trade Secrets for Designing with Style

How
(and Why)
to Use
This Book

A fabulous bedroom is part boudoir, part sanctuary. If you do any work there (even paying the bills), it's part home office. And if you retreat to the bedroom occasionally with afternoon tea and a magazine, it's partly your private living room, too.

How well does your bedroom work for you? If it's thoughtfully furnished and expressively decorated, the room should serve you as an inviting place to read, write letters, phone a friend, romance your partner, sprawl with a laptop, eat breakfast, or curl up to watch a video.

With ideas and guidance from the pros, you *can* make it happen, even if you aren't always confident in your decorating taste or ability.

WHO DREAMED UP THESE DESIGN IDEAS?

Most of the 100-plus tips, inspirational ideas, and tricks of the trade on these pages come from interior designers around the country. As a design writer (and a fan), I've spent the last decade quizzing them on the details of their work.

From all those interviews come the nuggets of design advice that pack this book. Indeed, all the designers mentioned on these pages were incredibly generous with their knowledge, and just as specific. (They had to be. If a designer recommended, say, a sheer bedroom curtain but couldn't offer a useful or intriguing way of dressing the window with it, you won't find him in this book. Because what good is advice that you can't take to the store?)

Still, there's a caveat: Occasionally, one tip seems to contradict another. That's because designers often disagree—for every decorator who loves whisper-white bedrooms, there's another who swears by oceanic-blue walls—and what looks glamorous in one bedroom may be impractical in others. In the end, it comes down to trusting your own instincts: just follow the tips that feel right for you.

THE ELEGANT AND EASY PREMISE

The Elegant and Easy approach to bedroom design is both forgiving and intuitive. It lets you decorate naturally and on impulse, as inspiration strikes (or as money flows in). It encourages you to spend wisely, and also to save money creatively.

That's the premise. Here's the promise:

If you try any five ideas from these pages, you will love your bedroom more.

It doesn't matter if your budget runs to $500 or $50,000, or if you live in an apartment or a house. Any five of these professional design "recipes," chosen from the heart and applied in any order, will make your bedroom more romantic, more serene, more sensual, more polished, or more vibrant—more of anything you wish, because *your* taste and *your* instincts are what guide you.

Here's what you won't need: grand plans, floor plans, or exquisitely educated taste. (Yes, that's what design profession-

How (and Why) to Use This Book

3

als bring to the table, but this book was written for the rest of us: people on modest budgets who must think, and decorate, for ourselves.) And let's be honest—you won't get a bedroom so lavish in every detail that magazine scouts knock on your door. Only serious money, and the services of an interior designer, can achieve such luxury.

But you *can* make your bedroom more beautiful and sybaritic with these tips from the professionals and an Elegant and Easy upgrade.

To that end, I wish you joyous decorating and the bedroom of your dreams.

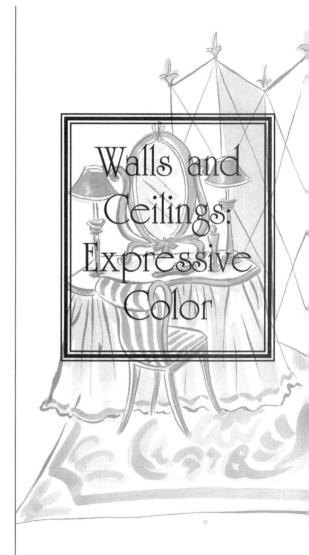

Walls and Ceilings: Expressive Color

When architects design a house or an apartment, they usually save the best of everything—light, views, expansiveness—for semipublic spaces like the living room. As a result, a bedroom may get the architectural leftovers: rear windows, or a lower ceiling, or less square footage than one might like. Sometimes it is full of charm regardless. Other times you have to add that charm yourself—through savvy decorating and wise design.

Your greatest tool, in such cases, is color. And the best place to use it is on walls (and, sometimes, the ceiling). "You have to make the bedroom so warm, so dramatic, that it becomes your interior garden," says Nan Lee, partner in the New York design and architecture firm Lee/Wimpenny.

Lean toward colors that feel serene to you. If white springs to mind, make sure you love it enough to create an entire off-white palette throughout the room—not only pale sepia walls, for example, but also ivory curtains, a camel-colored rug, snowy sheets, Battenberg lace pillows. One chain of decorating stores, Janovic/Plaza, claims to stock more than 1,000 shades of off-white paint. At the very least, choose one for walls, one for the ceiling, and one for trim to give the room contrast and dimension.

But white is far from the only suitable or restful color for bedrooms. Borrow from nature, which rarely errs. Imagine a bedroom painted in any of the following:

- Blue: either a delicate sky shade or cornflower.

- Pink: any hue from pink-white peony to coral.

- Grape green or sage green.

- Chocolate!

As New York designer Craig Raywood puts it, "Anything drawn from nature is a neutral." Indeed, there's only one caveat: in the bedroom, avoid colors that make your heart race, like purple and red.

The colors suggested in this chapter are paint shades that real interior designers have used themselves, with great success. If a color sounds too intense for your taste, check out the paint chip anyway—just knowing that a professional likes it may embolden your own choices.

Finally, take a tip from San Francisco designer Joan Malter Osburn, who knows how unnerving it can be to stray far from the safety of white. When looking at strips of paint samples from big manufacturers like Benjamin Moore or Pratt & Lambert, Osburn advises, focus on the sample that's third from the top.

"If you go higher, you lose the character of the color," she says, "and if you go lower, it's often too intense. For most people, the third chip just seems very comfortable."

A note on paint

The most practical paint is latex, not oil. It dries fast, cleans up with water, and doesn't offend the environment. Use an eggshell finish on walls, semigloss on woodwork.

Caution: Paint in rich, deep colors, particularly red, is saturated with pigment. When you wash dirt off a wall painted in eggshell latex, the red pigment may lift away, too, leaving a permanent mark.

Here are three solutions, none perfect: (1) Use eggshell latex anyway, because it looks good. Clean lightly with a sponge, which is less abrasive than cloth. (2) Use semigloss paint. It stands up well to cleaning, but you must have near-perfect walls, as the sheen highlights flaws. (3) For imperfect walls that require frequent cleaning—if you have children, say—consider oil paint.

THE NATURAL NEUTRALS

Neutral colors can have surprising depth. For an evocative, enveloping taupe, choose Benjamin Moore HC-91 or HC-92, suggests Jeffrey Goodman of the L.A. design firm Goodman Charlton. For trim, try Benjamin Moore no. 961 or 954, both taupe-y shades of off-white. For accent colors (in flowers, fabrics, even a single vase), Goodman suggests olive green and chartreuse.

Tip: Natural sisal carpeting will look beautiful in this room. Layer smaller wool rugs over it to accommodate bare feet.

AMBERING THE WALLPAPER

Bring instant nostalgia to new bedroom wallpaper by tinting it with tea. This recipe is from Brooklyn, NY, designer Corey Nicholas of the firm Interior Sense:

Wet a handful of Tetley teabags in a bowl of warm water. Transfer them to a piece of cheesecloth, and tie the cheesecloth closed, so tea leaves can't escape. Rub the cheesecloth package all over the wallpaper, varying your strokes: pounce, scour, sweep, "as if you're cleaning the wall," says Nicholas.

Walls and Ceilings: Expressive Color

9

Tip: After tea-dyeing, Nicholas peels back the paper's corners to further evoke antiquity. Peeled by an amateur, the paper can look shabby—but if your paper has started to peel on its own, try tea-dyeing as a temporary or permanent solution.

IMPLY THE SKY

Keep a white-walled bedroom from looking pallid by lending color to the ceiling. Blue is widely considered relaxing, so consider one of the light blues that the Victorians applied to porch ceilings—a tradition that remains strong today and will remind you of being outdoors.

Here are four shades to test, all historically appropriate and all Benjamin Moore: no. 723, 730, 674, and, with a touch more green in it, 660.

ENSCONCED IN PATTERN

Don't fight the confines of a tiny bedroom—play up its intimacy, says Lee Bierly of the Boston design firm Bierly-Drake. Paper the walls in one of three classic patterns: cabbage roses, toile, or a stripe. "Stripes give you the feeling of being inside a tent," says Bierly. A bonus: With patterned walls, you'll need fewer pictures.

Paper the ceiling, too, if it's low, angled, or oddly shaped. Enveloped by pattern, you'll barely notice where the walls stop and the ceiling starts.

BORROW ROMANCE FROM A RUG

Aubusson rugs, designed in eighteenth-century France with leaves, roses, and beautiful flourishes, look exquisite in bedrooms. But if, like most people, you cannot afford one, try drawing your wall and ceiling colors from this Aubusson paint palette, created by Benjamin Moore's color marketing consultant, Kenneth X. Charbonneau. (All paint shades are Benjamin Moore.)

Deep rose Aubusson: 1309 (red rose), 1078 (deep tan), 1095 (ivory), 1096 (pale tan), 1294 (deep muted rose), 1293(dusty rose).

Gold and rose Aubusson: 1300 (wine red), 1102 (breathy tan), 1101 (bone), 1147 (honey brown), 1125 (dark paperbag).

COLORS FROM THE FIELDS

The golden-apple colors recommended by Bonnie Rosser Krims in her paint-savvy book *The Perfect Palette* (Warner Books) produce a meditative bedroom that's quietly in tune with nature. For example, paint the walls apple yellow (Benjamin Moore no. 170), and use sage green (Benjamin Moore no. 495) in the hall just outside. (They're just as good reversed.) For an adjoining bath, try beige with just a breath of green in it (Benjamin Moore no. 1037).

Tip: Krims' book, which shows dozens
of her favorite paint colors right on the page,
may save you some money in trial-and-error testing.

THE PERFECT WHITE

Certain shades of white work so well on moldings (not to mention walls and ceilings) that designers return to them on every job. Look at paint chips for White Dove, Linen White, and no. 925, all Benjamin Moore, and simply choose one you like best. All will look lovely in a bedroom.

THE COLORS OF WARMTH

Designer Barbara Southerland loves these colors for a bedroom that is both delicate and crisp (or for people aware of both their masculine and their feminine sides):

Walls: Benjamin Moore no. 085, a pale peach that's flattering to most people.

Walls of adjacent hall or bath: Benjamin Moore no. 086, a brighter shade of peach.

Woodwork: Benjamin Moore's White Dove, a warm white.

To extend the palette, have the bedskirt and curtains made from a chintz in softly faded colors, buy a white mattelassé bedcover (available from bedding catalogs), and consider upholstering one good reading chair in apricot with charcoal-gray welting.

GRAY-FLANNEL PAINT

For a tailored bedroom, Southerland prescribes the following:

Walls: Benjamin Moore no. 1488, a medium charcoal gray.

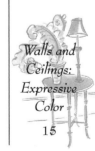

Walls and Ceilings: Expressive Color

Woodwork: Benjamin Moore's Atrium White, a clean, bright white.

Among her decorating suggestions: Hang curtains in a yellow and gray stripe, upholster a chaise longue in yellow, and invest in four to six architectural engravings in black or gilt frames.

A SERENE PALETTE

Blue, especially if warmed by undertones of red, is always serene in a bedroom. "It's a spa color, a sky color, a spiritual color," says San Francisco designer Joan Malter Osburn. Among her favorites:

- Benjamin Moore no. 815. May shift from lilac to a deeper hue as the daylight changes.

- Benjamin Moore no. 822. A lilac that's almost gray-blue.

- Benjamin Moore no. 647. Fresh blue-green, comprising many pigments, which makes it change hue as the light changes around it.

Paint the ceiling white, says Osburn. Alternatively, use any one blue on the walls, any other on the ceiling.

CHOCOLATE, STONE, CAFÉ AU LAIT

The legendary decorator Billy Baldwin made brown rooms chic and famous; for sparkle, he added brass accents in his bookshelves and lamps. Many designers still favor brown. In Washington, DC, designer Barry Dixon often uses it in small bedrooms, applying it not only to walls but to ceilings. "When you unify all the surfaces with a dark color, you lose sight of the stop-and-start points and shadows that reveal the boundaries of the room," Dixon says.

His five favorite shades:

- Benjamin Moore no. 999. "The color of dark stone."

- Benjamin Moore no. 1000. A dark brown-taupe.

- Benjamin Moore no. 1238. "Semisweet chocolate."

- Benjamin Moore no. 1232. "True milk chocolate."

- Benjamin Moore HC-69. A muted brown (and a historic color) with green-gray undertones.

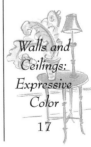

Fabrics in yellow, red, and royal or French blue work beautifully with brown walls.

*Tip: One brown room is perfect;
two is overkill.*

NATURAL COLORS, UNUSUAL DEPTH

Donald Kaufman Color paints are revered among designers for their subtle, complex, pigment-rich colors, many drawn from nature. New York designer DD Allen, a partner in Pierce Allen, created this soothing Donald Kaufman palette for bedrooms:

Walls: DKC 30, a soft buttery yellow.

Adjoining hall or bath: DKC 25, part olive, part stone.

Small accent areas, like the interior of a niche: DKC 26, a darker velvety olive.

Ceilings and trim: DKC 5, a white that Allen calls "not too creamy, not too stark."

Tip: Donald Kaufman Color swatches must be purchased by mail; at 4 by 8 inches, they are about the largest in the business, which makes them worth the price. The paint, too, is sold by mail, or in concentrates that your local paint store can mix up, for a fee. Call (201) 568-2226 for swatches, paint, and information.

PALE AND ELUSIVE HUES

Another DD Allen palette for the bedroom has even more restraint. These colors look fresh, yet are intriguingly hard to define:

Walls: DKC 11, an extremely pale green-gray.

Adjoining hall or bath: DKC 2, a green-yellow so pale it barely registers as a color.

Small accent areas: DKC 33, a pale aqua tinged with gray.

Ceilings and trim: DKC 5, a soft white.

For information on DKC paints and swatches, call (201) 568-2226.

Walls and
Ceilings:
Expressive
Color

19

PAINT IN SAMPLE SIZES

Test-drive paint colors for your bedroom walls by ordering 4-ounce sample jars in the mail. Adler Brothers, a Providence, RI, hardware and decorating firm, sells more than 1,000 Pratt & Lambert color samples for $2 a jar. (A quart, by contrast, can cost $10 or $15, and is far more than you need for a test.) Pratt & Lambert paint strips can be found at most paint stores. For more information, call Adler Brothers at (401) 421-5157; ask for the paint department.

RECIPE FOR A GLAZED WALL

When paint is mixed with glazing medium and applied in layers of different colors, the walls look lovely, mottled and rich. But for all the do-it-yourself books on glazing, it's messy and pricey to mix precisely the colors you want.

Solution: Glaze recipes from art•decor. This California firm offers clear instructions on how to achieve specific colors like slate, parchment, burnt copper, or stone; you pay $20 for the recipe, which includes the names of paint shades, the proportions, and exact directions for two translucent coats of glaze.

Tip: Ask a major fabric store to recommend a workroom or
decorator to help with the job.

The firm will also create a glaze recipe to match, say, a beloved sweater (about $45).

For a brochure, contact art•decor, 765 Cedar Street, Berkeley, CA 94710; tel. (510) 527-3904.

THE WELL-DRESSED WALL

If noise from traffic or neighbors disturbs your peace in the bedroom, muffle it: cover the walls with fabric. Your choices:

- Hire a fabric workroom or wall upholsterer. An expert will apply padded and fabric-wrapped panels to your walls or frame out the wall with wood strips to which the fabric is staple-gunned. "It need not be all over the room," says Chicago designer Janet Schirn. "You can upholster just the wall that's between you and the noise, or the wall behind your bed."

- Curtain the wall instead; it's easier and soft-looking. The traditional method is to affix a brass rod under the crown molding, another above the baseboard; the fabric, tightly gathered, is held taut between the two. For extra soundproofing, staple batting up first.

Tip: *The trim should look the same on both sides,*
so that you can coax it around corners by folding it into a right angle.

EVOKE PROVENCE

To make a diminutive bedroom feel airy, paint everything—walls, ceiling, doors, and trim—in Benjamin Moore no. 957, which Austin designer Hortensia Vitali calls the color of straw. It also happens to be the perfect backdrop for French country furniture and fabrics.

ADD DRESSMAKER DETAILS

If you are wallpapering a bedroom, give it a custom signature with subtle trimmings. Buy gimp or flat braid in a color that matches, or relates to, the *backdrop* color of the wallpaper. Using a glue gun (from craft and stationery stores), attach the trim along the four edges of each wall, right where the wallpaper meets the molding or stops at a corner. When you are finished, every wall will be framed with trim. "It looks very customized and expensive," says New York designer Marshall Watson.

GILDING WITH A TWIST

Kim DePole, a New York designer, is enchanted with Chinese joss papers—rectangles of marigold- or parchment-colored paper adorned with irregular squares of gold leaf. Joss papers can be found in department stores in the Chinatown section of any city; they are meant as temple offerings, but DePole prefers to glue them up in rows, as wallpaper borders over

painted walls. Apply one row under the crown moldings, and a second, if desired, above the baseboards.

A $3.50 package of joss papers contains about 100 sheets; calculate the number of packs based on the size of your room and the paper size you choose. DePole buys them roughly index-card size; they also come about 6 by 8 inches. The papers are not always square; trim edges to make them even, if necessary. Now, with blue masking tape (it's gentler to the paint on your walls), mask off the strip of wall where the papers will go. Apply Modpodge, a glue found at arts and crafts supply stores, to the wall; affix the papers. Then brush Modpodge (which also works as a sealer) over the squares and remove the blue tape.

Source: Pearl River Mart in New York sells joss papers under the name "tea paper" on its website: www.pearlriver-.com.

INSIDE A CLOUD

For atmospheric romance, try violet walls with nearly pure white trim. Pratt & Lambert's Violet Harmony, no. 1103, is the kind of lavender you might find in a perfect sunset. Benjamin Moore's Decorators White on the woodwork creates a cloud-white contrast.

Bedroom
Windows

$\mathcal{D}$arkness on Sunday mornings. Bright sun on Monday. Privacy from the neighbors, but also a view— we do ask a lot of our bedroom cur-tains. And it helps, of course, if they have a romantic or peaceful quality that makes the bedroom more of a sanctuary.

Not every trade secret in this chapter can meet all these requirements. Depending on your needs, you may have to (a) prioritize or (b) combine treatments—using, for example, an opaque shade behind a sheer drapery.

Now for the easy part: You can dress a bedroom window with less effort than a window in a living or dining room. Consider a blowsy length of gauze tossed over a rod: in the living room, it can look insubstantial, but in the bedroom, it suggests a veil. Delicacy works in the privacy of a bedroom, and delicate fabrics (think linen, lace, and sheers) are often reasonably priced.

Simplicity works, too. A surprising number of houses and apartments by top designers have bedroom windows dressed only in pristine white schoolhouse shades, the kind you may recall from your third-grade classroom. If the shades are cus-tom-made for a tailored fit, you'll find that the understate-ment works.

Try not to overcoordinate. If you make curtains to match your patterned sheets, the room will look predictable—and after a while you'll tune out that gorgeous pattern. Let window treatments stand on their own. If you still crave co-ordination, do something overscaled and unexpected: cut an 18-inch-high band from the patterned sheets and sew it across the base of starched white curtains. You'll have broken out of a formula, and the details of your decorating will stand out the better for it.

CAPTURE SUNLIGHT

Dress up a fabric-covered valance or fabric shades by sewing chandelier crystals along the bottom edge, suggests New York designer Wilbert Louis Shaw. They'll catch the sunlight (or even lamplight) prismatically. Flea market dealers who specialize in antique lighting fixtures often have boxes full of old crystals lying around; you may be able to scoop them up for $1 apiece.

Tip: Measure carefully to get the spacing right; the crystals are an eye-catcher, so any irregularity will be noticed.

CUSTOMIZE A SHADE PULL

Old-fashioned schoolhouse shades, perenially in style because of their unvarnished simplicity, often have a round pull dangling from a string. Follow the example of New York designer Carl D'Aquino and replace the pull with something sculptural and high touch. For one client, D'Aquino had a miniature abstract sculpture made by an artist, but you might also use a pendant, a baby's gold bangle, or a single chandelier crystal that toys with the light.

Bedroom Windows

Or find a department store in your local Chinatown, and look for the round jade carvings, like medallions, that dangle from black cords—a bargain at about $10, and eminently suitable for shades.

SLEEPING LATE

Does the morning sun make it difficult for you to sleep until brunch? If so, your window treatments aren't amply tailored to your needs. Have curtains made with a blackout lining to keep the room dark, or install a blackout shade behind the curtains you already have. And don't let the word *blackout* intimidate you: the lining you see is traditionally white (though it can be any other color you choose).

UPSIDE-DOWN SHADES

Sometimes it's not sun but the curiosity of neighbors that you wish to thwart. To create privacy without vanquishing the sunlight, San Francisco designer Joan Malter Osburn likes simple white shades that pull up from the bottom. (Any window-treatment specialist can install shades this way.) When halfway up, they grant privacy while giving you a glimpse of the sky.

ANCHOR A DRAPERY

For an elegant but economical window treatment, designer Michael Buchanan, of New York's Goralnick★Buchanan, installed matchstick blinds in a client's window frame and hung a pair of heavy starched white linen panels in front. Sunlight could slip through the matchstick blinds, but when the linen drapery was drawn, the bedroom had privacy.

Neither the blinds nor the linen was costly—but both looked it, Buchanan says, because of one key detail: He gave the floor-length linen curtains an ultra-deep hem. He advises a hem of 14 inches if your ceiling feels low, 20 inches if it's high, or anywhere between that looks right to your eye.

INSTALL A PAPER COLUMN

Ennoble a skimpy window: flank it with trompe l'oeil wallpaper columns, suggests designer Margot Gunther of the New York firm Gunther-Watson. Make the columns a few inches shorter than the ceiling so that the curtain rod, mounted close to ceiling height, will appear to rest on the capitals (the highly ornamented column tops). Drape gauze or sheer fabric over the rod, letting the fabric fall to the

ground. "The look is right out of *A Midsummer Night's Dream*," Gunther says.

Tape the columns up first so you can play with the positioning until it looks right.

Source: Wallpaper columns by Gramercy are 13 inches wide and come in three pieces—column, base, and capital—so you can control the height. For retailers and other information, call (800) 988-7775.

MOONLIT SPLENDOR

Play up the after-dark splendor of a light-deprived bedroom: hang royal- or midnight-blue velvet draperies, to evoke a twilit sky. Sew fake pearls to the velvet in any pattern you like (spacing them at regular intervals is probably simplest). "The pearls will look luminescent and will remind you of stars," says Chicago designer Janet Schirn.

Tip: For midnight-blue walls, design writer Terry Trucco swears by Benjamin Moore no. 826.

CURTAINS ON CONSIGNMENT

Have you ever coveted the curtains in a designer showhouse? They sometimes end up in curtain consignment stores, like The Curtain Exchange in New Orleans. (So do draperies created for wealthy clients who've decided to redecorate.) The Curtain Exchange charges roughly one-third the original cost, and, most important, works by mail. You send photos of your bedroom windows, measurements, and any relevant paint chips, and the Curtain Exchange will send you Polaroid photos of curtains—which you can then try on approval. (Note that some of the draperies are newly designed by the owners of the shop.)

For more information, contact The Curtain Exchange, 3947 Magazine Street, New Orleans, LA 70115; tel. (504) 897-2444.

THE CURTAIN AND THE SHELF

The editors of *Better Homes and Gardens* devised a graceful window treatment that married a petite drapery to a display shelf. It appeared in a kitchen, but is here adapted to a bedroom.

Buy two ready-made wood brackets (the kind that can support a shelf) from a lumberyard or Home Depot. Mount

Bedroom Windows

them on either side of the window, making them flush with the top of the casing (or higher, if you want the illusion of a taller ceiling). Cut a shelf as deep as the brackets and set it on top. Edge it with molding, if desired. Paint the shelf and brackets white.

Now set a slim tension rod (from any hardware or fabric store) between the brackets. Float a lightweight, floor-length sheer from the rod. Set a few lovely objects or vases on the shelf. It will make a handsome display and draw the eye up, implying height.

TYING THE KNOT

Sheer drapery can be downright ravishing when treated like a bridal veil. For maximum effect, Benjamin Noriega-Ortiz, a New York designer, likes to contrast sheer organza with a stark, architectural rod, as follows:

Run a white-painted wood dowel across the *entire* window wall, mounting the dowel directly to the ceiling so it looks more like an urban-loft pipe fitting than a curtain rod. (A good window-treatment or decorating store can supply the ceiling-mount hardware.) Now, buy a length of white organza that is twice the height of the wall plus 18 extra inches, and slightly wider than the window. (Sheer fabrics run wide, to spare you from visible seams.)

Bedroom
Windows

35

Here's the bridal-veil part: Dress up the organza by having it piped on all four edges with white silk cord. Now toss it over the rod like a giant scarf, so the back just kisses the floor and the front puddles. Tie the front of the curtain in a big, loose knot slightly below eye level. The result is ravishing.

MIX COLORS AND LIGHT

Craig Raywood, a New York designer, not only uses sheers in colors—he layers them, as if mixing translucent paints. Strong sunlight creates a third color as it penetrates the two fabrics, and the double layer gives you more privacy.

Raywood recently bought iridescent silk taffeta in amethyst and amber and sewed the two layers together at the top before hanging. As the fabrics drape, they separate slightly, so you can tell two colors are interacting. You might also do navy over cream, says Raywood, or ivory over taupe; the colors need not be vibrant to look good. "Decide if you want the effect to be subtle or a standout—then choose your colors," he advises.

Tip: Hang simply, without much gathering, from any curtain hardware you like that won't steal the show.

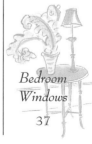

Bedroom Windows

CLEAN AND CLASSIC

Nothing looks as sleek and architectural as 2-inch wood blinds. Match the color of the slats to your floorboards, or order them in white. Choose black tapes (for drama) or white cords (which are barely visible) for a clean contemporary look. Avoid the lure of brightly colored tapes and cords; as little samples they may look cheerful, but they'll honk for attention on your blinds.

Have the blinds mounted inside, not outside, the window frame. It requires a custom job, but adds tremendous polish to a room.

LET THE WINDOW REIGN

Even the most elaborate curtains can work to your detriment if they obscure any of the glass behind them. Far too many expensive custom valances hang low over the top of the window, wiping out part of the sky.

Set your curtains high and wide so they cover the casing, or window trim, but not the glass. This will not only liberate your view but will increase the room's sense of height and scale.

CONQUER AN AIRSHAFT VIEW

Many apartment dwellers know the plight of a bedroom window that faces a brick wall. To veil this dreary view without totally obscuring the window, Marshall Watson, a New York designer, recommends a semisheer curtain of burnt velvet. This beautiful material is part solid velvet and part sheer, where the nap was burned away in a pattern. Light sneaks through, but your gaze stops at the design instead of traveling past it to the wall outside.

SUNLIGHT BY REMOTE CONTROL

Imagine not having to get out of bed to raise the blinds—or to lower them, if you want to sleep late. Motorized blinds, which work by remote control, are an intoxicating luxury. For one New York couple, designer Benjamin Noriega-Ortiz installed motorized white opaque shades (called blackout shades) behind gauzy Roman blinds. Dressing for bed, his clients would click to lower the blackout shades; in bed, with the lights out, they would click to raise them, revealing the sparkle of New York's nighttime skyline. Finally, at daybreak, husband or wife would wake up, grab the remote, lower the shades against the sun, and go back to sleep.

Bedroom
Windows

Yes, it's a luxury, but worth pricing, as more manufacturers catch on. And the possibilities are tantalizing. "Curtains, blinds, anything that's on a window can be motorized," says Steven Schulman of Manhattan Shade & Glass. (Go to a window-covering specialist, not a hardware store.) Consider it a worthy investment if your bed is a command center for reading, writing, talking on the phone, and relaxing.

DRESS UP A SKINNY DORMER

When curtaining a dormer window, you're often dealing with an undersize window in a narrow niche. Let your drapery, at least, create a sense of generosity. Buy sheer fabric in a light, neutral color (or use tulle from a store that sells bridal fabrics). Install the rod above the window at the highest possible point of the dormer wall. Make the curtain three times as wide as the dormer niche, and let it float all the way to the floor. The cascade of fabric creates architectural stature and still admits light.

THE LUXURIOUS WINDOW PERCH

If you are fortunate enough to have a window seat, give it the same respect you pay your living room sofa. First, hang shades or curtains in a neutral color and style, so your window seat will be the star. Have the seat cushion made fat—New York upholsterer Jeff Alexander recommends a 3- to 4-inch thickness with a crown, or a graceful bulge, in the middle. Run contrasting welting or moss fringe along the seams. Order a bolster for either end.

Bedroom Windows

CHAPTER 3

The Glorious Bed (and Bedding)

A dream bed is yours for life. Buy it to fit your dramatic, romantic fantasies, not to suit a modest bedroom. After all, you may move—but the bed is yours forever.

Indeed, the only reason not to invest in a splendid bed is because you can't afford it yet. In that case, don't settle for second best. Consider a more moderate splurge on linens, mosquito netting, or a flea-market headboard you can transform with paint. The upgrade will instantly show, the bed will look richer, and the room will beckon like a private sanctuary.

Many people are understandably anxious about planting an oversize bed (like a huge four-poster, or an opium bed with its red lacquer "roof") in a small bedroom. But there's a trick to making these marriages flourish: just avoid bed hangings or canopies that obstruct your view. If you crave a canopy, be restrained—drape *sheer* fabric across the top of the frame. It won't block your view, and the magnificent bed could make the room around it look larger.

Finally, remember that quality is something you can feel, not just see. Spend money on a good mattress. Buy a down-filled duvet (watch the catalogs for sales). Replace your pillows if the goosedown inside them has flattened, and encase them in pillow protectors. These things are as important as pretty sheets, and they can make your bed the most restorative place in your home.

THE POWER OF WHITE PAINT

When the late Sister Parish was newly married, her rich and highly starched mother-in-law presented her with an heirloom: a magnificent suite of ebony furniture. Parish, in search of simplicity, promptly painted it white. Her relatives were appalled, but Parish, not yet a decorator, knew she was on to something. The lesson? If you can't afford a stunning four-poster antique bed, buy a battered flea-market specimen with good lines. Sand, prime, and paint white. It will reign in your bedroom like a bride.

Tip: For visual continuity,
do this to a second piece of furniture,
too, such as a tall bureau
or wooden chair.

A SENSUOUS TOUCH

"What makes a bed sexy is a mix of different textures," says New York designer Craig Raywood. When buying throws, commissioning pillows from an upholsterer, ordering spreads or bed hangings, or reupholstering a padded headboard, try to use at least one sensual material that will engage your sense of touch. For instance: fur pillows (made from an old thrift-shop coat), a cashmere or mohair throw, a suede headboard, or draperies of fine wool or silk.

The
Glorious
Bed (and
Bedding)

47

DESIGN PURITY

A Shaker-style bed, with its four tall, tapering posts, is a classic design that looks elegant no matter where it's placed—a romantic cottage or a minimalist condominium. Most Shaker beds are done in natural wood tones, but the lines of these beds are so lean and lanky that they look great in black. Many stores and catalogs carry this style—which,

incidentally, is superb for small bedrooms. A Shaker bed is big enough to trick your mind's eye into perceiving a bigger room, yet it takes up almost no visual space. To keep this airy effect, don't add a dust skirt or fabric canopy; by obstructing your view, they'll make the room feel crowded.

RESHAPE THE BED

If you are wedded to sleeping in a king-size bed, you've probably struggled with the awkward-looking geometry—a big

square mattress, hulking in a rectangular room. "Put a bench or a little sofa at the foot of the bed," advises designer Michael Buchanan of Goralnick★Buchanan in New York. "It changes the bed's proportion from a square to a rectangle, and makes it work."

Tip: To break up the blank expanse of the bed's surface, drape a beautiful throw across it.

HINT AT A CANOPY

Even without a four-poster, you can sleep under a canopy of sorts by suspending a long "scarf" of sheer fabric from the ceiling.

You'll need an inexpensive sheer material and two white-painted wood dowels about 2 inches longer than the fabric's width. Hang the dowels a foot or so from the ceiling, one at each end of the bed. (Trust your eye; the room's size and height will influence how high the veil should hang.)

Now toss the sheer across the rods like a scarf, so it acts as a roof over your pillows and pools on the floor at both ends.

Tip: *To hang a dowel, affix an eye to either end.*
(An eye is a little metal circle attached to a screw, as in the
hook-and-eye lock on an old screen door.) Have two cup-hooks
screwed, and possibly glued, into the ceiling. Suspend the dowel with
nylon fishing line from the hardware store.

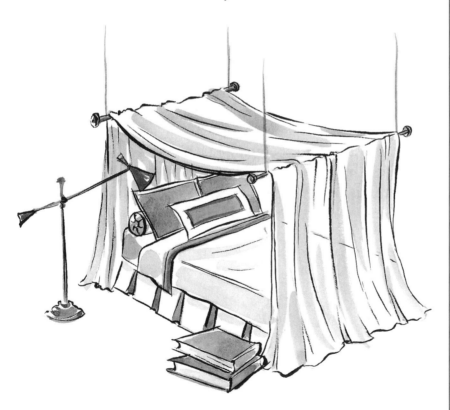

THE FLOATING BED

In an impossibly small bedroom he calls "dollhouse-sized," Washington, DC, designer Barry Dixon created a kind of temple to sleep: he floated a king-size bed in the center of room, like an island. "Because it was free-floating, you didn't feel crowded," he says.

What made it work? Dixon erased boundaries by saturating walls, drapery, chair upholstery, and the bedskirt in a single toile de Jouy fabric. The top of the bed, however, he draped with a natural-color linen spread—no pattern. "Your eye goes straight to the one different thing," he explains.

For a less costly version, reverse the approach: Use an inexpensive, solid-color fabric for curtains, upholstery, and bedskirt, and paint walls to match. Now, in your one splurge, buy a bedcover of some exquisite fabric. (Just as a starting point, imagine walls and fabrics in a restful taupe, and a bedcovering of scarlet silk.)

EXPLORE A NEW ANGLE

A visual trick for small bedrooms: Angle the bed out from a corner. This works particularly well with a four-poster, and creates new, triangular spaces that can dispel the boxed-in feeling of a little room. To dispel shadows in the corner behind the bed, place a fabric-covered, standing screen there.

The ideal position: an angled bed with a direct view of the window. "That orientation means you're looking from a small area into a large outdoor space," says designer Barry Dixon.

Tip: If you can't angle the bed, try this space-expanding tactic with an armchair or desk.

FLAUNT GOOD LEGS

If your bed has attractive legs, don't bother with a bedskirt. It's a common designer trick: in small rooms, leave more of the floor exposed, and the space will appear larger. You can apply this to satellite furnishings, too, buying bureaus or armoires that stand on legs instead of platforms. Just don't do this with every piece, or the room will look, as designers say, leggy.

HEIGHTEN THE EXPERIENCE

A bed with a high mattress has a regal, almost Southern feeling, but it usually requires the purchase of an antique.

However, you can cheat: Purchase the Bed Rizer, a set of four tall legs you can attach to a standard metal frame.

Having done this, you'll find your present bedskirt too short. To get an 18-inch or 21-inch skirt (depending on the Bed Rizer legs you order), see the Bed Rizer catalog or engage a slipcover workshop or a bedding catalog that does custom work. Make the skirt tailored or box-pleated—not a cascade of fussy ruffles.

For information, contact Bed Rizer, 736 Federal Street, Davenport, IA 52803; tel. (800) 513-1987, or www.bedrizer.com.

Tip: If you haven't done so already,
now's the time to buy those under-bed storage boxes.

THE LIBRARY BED

To create a bedroom or guest room that doubles as a study, buy an antique (or reproduction) sleigh bed or daybed, and place it sideways against the wall. Properly made up, it will look like an elegant sofa, but it also sleeps two. Designer Michael Buchanan shares his tricks for making this work:

- Buy a full-size, not a queen-size, daybed.

- Have three firm pillows made to build up the back of the bed; use foam, or a combination of foam and down. Make them 8 to 10 inches deep, 24 inches tall, and wide enough so that they line up from the head of the bed to the foot.

The Glorious Bed (and Bedding)

- Pile on a collection of gorgeous throw pillows.

- Add bed hangings that will drape loosely behind the bed and slightly over its sides, thus visually diminishing its depth. The drapery can can be as simple as mosquito netting (see the Mombasa catalog listed in Chapter 6), or you can have something custom-made. Advises Buchanan: "Edge the drapery with trim so it looks finished."

PUT PILLOWS IN FANCY DRESS

To instantly upgrade your bed, slip all of your pillows into standard-size shams—pillowcases that are framed by a flange, or extra fabric edging, on all four sides. They'll look classier, and you can sleep on them every night.

Layer at least four shams onto a full- or queen-size bed. Buy them tailored (with a flat flange) for a sophisticated look.

THE LUXE OF LINEN

The rich are different from you and me: their beds are often clothed in crisp, hand-laundered linen sheets. Linen has a lovely weight to it, and feels cooler and more substantial than cotton. After many launderings, it's also surprisingly soft. But these sheets can cost hundreds of dollars apiece and can rarely be tossed in the dryer, making them inconvenient for anyone without servants.

But—even on a budget—you can afford the pleasure of linen shams. They'll wrinkle, but being pillowcases, they're a cinch to wash and iron. The moral: A touch of luxury is often enough.

THE SAFARI BED

Designer and author Tricia Foley, who specializes in romantic white rooms, often drapes beds with mosquito netting.

Rather than enclose a bed completely, Foley sometimes takes the two bottom corners of the net's single opening and lifts them high and to the sides, creating a graceful and regal entry into the space beneath the net.

Foley's favorite source is Mombasa (see Chapter 6), which sells numerous styles; the Majesty net comes closest to the Foley technique. Bedding catalogs like Garnet Hill and stores like Pier 1 have also discovered netting, so it should not be hard to find.

INITIAL YOUR LINENS

Take the extra step of having your shams and duvet cover monogrammed, says Barbara Southerland, a designer in Greenville, NC, and New York. It's one of those touches that doesn't cost much but looks incredibly rich. For monogram-mers, check the Yellow Pages under *M*, or order through a bedding catalog (see Chapter 6) that offers the service.

DRESS THE BED WISELY

A completely new wardrobe for your bed can cost $500 or more once you've chosen the sheets, shams, duvet cover, bed-skirt, and a neckroll or two. The trick to containing costs is to buy at least half the basics—like bottom sheets, duvet cover, and bedskirt—in solid neutral colors and high thread counts, so they'll look good (and last) for a number of years. Indulge in pattern for shams, top sheets, and ornamental pillows. Now, when you want a change, you won't have to replace your entire linen closet.

SCENTS AND BREEZES

Spray the underside of your pillow with a light cologne. Try a lavender scent: it's widely used to promote both sleep and serenity.

And while indulging in scent, remember the importance of fresh air. Open a window. Run an air purifier. Install a ceiling fan and keep the air moving around your bed.

AN ELEMENT OF RELAXATION

For an extra element of comfort in bed, buy a neckroll and a pretty cover for it. Whether you're leaning back or lying down, it cradles the neck quite nicely. Most neckrolls are foam- or feather-filled, but for firm, malleable support, try one filled with buckwheat hulls (from a store with a wide selection of bedding).

THE SPIRITUAL BED

If you are intrigued by feng shui, the ancient Chinese art of designing rooms for a harmonious flow of energy, why not borrow a few of its precepts when positioning the bed? These are adapted from *The Feng Shui House Book* by Gina Lazenby (Watson-Guptill), which is well worth the price of the photos alone:

- Place the bed so it backs up to a wall and has a clear view of the door but is not directly facing the doorway. This is considered a secure position that keeps you out of the way of *chi* (energy) flowing into the room.

- Don't site your bed under a beam. If the beam can't be avoided, soften the effect with a fabric canopy or mosquito netting.

- If you own an armoire with mirrored doors, make sure you can't see your own reflection when you're in bed.

- Replace your mattress as soon as you begin an important new relationship.

A HEADBOARD OF STATURE

To make a monumental "antique" headboard, New York designer Kim DePole shops salvage yards for beautiful old doors and lines up two or three behind a client's bed. (The doors should look closely related, though not necessarily identical; a pair of pocket doors, the old-fashioned kind that slide apart and disappear within the walls, would be ideal.) Use enough doors so that the headboard is slightly wider than the bed, "to engage the sidetables," says DePole. Have a carpenter affix the doors to the wall.

Tip: You can align the tops of the doors
by having them affixed
at different heights from the floor.

The
Glorious
Bed (and
Bedding)

THE VICTORIAN BED

Few things are as pretty as a lacy iron bedstead, painted white. But if you simply paint a flea-market find, it can end up looking too new. Mary Baltz, a contributing editor for *Victoria* magazine, offers her recipe for painting and antiquing an old iron bed:

After cleaning and priming with metal primer, paint the bed with Benjamin Moore's White Dove latex paint in an eggshell finish.

When it dries, apply Kiwi brown shoe polish (the cake kind, from a tin) with a soft, clean piece of flannel. It goes a long way, so use only a small dab on the flannel. (Apply less polish to the raised decorations than you do to the straight iron bars.) As you spread the polish around, says Baltz, it begins to "take," and once dry, it won't rub off.

The result: a virgin-white bed with a blush of sepia, like something brought to life from a vintage photograph.

Bedroom Furniture in Supporting Roles

*Y*es, the bed is the centerpiece. But to customize the bedroom to your waking hours, pay attention to the attendant furnishings—bureaus, bedside tables, chairs, armoires, rugs, shelves, perhaps even a desk. Well chosen, these pieces make it easy, even inviting, to keep your papers organized, store out-of-season clothes, or retreat with lunch and a good novel to the sanctuary of your bedroom.

So many rules that govern the bedroom are not only outdated but a bit stifling. Why are nightstands designed as squat, matching oblongs? Why must a dressing table be kidney-shaped and flounced? And why can't a tiny bedroom be glorified, rather than diminished, by a magnificent 7-foot-high armoire?

Let's try some looser rules. Like this one from Cheryl MacLachlan, author of *Bringing It Home: England* (Clarkson Potter): "If you yearn to make your bedroom a retreat," she writes, "it should offer at least one option to the bed as a place to relax." It's such a simple point, but imagine your bedroom with a chaise or armchair for reading, an accommodating little table nearby, and an adjustable light.

These are the kinds of furnishings, along with storage pieces, that can make a bedroom both beautiful and multipurpose—a real daytime retreat. The bonus: A bedroom that welcomes you for reading, noshing, or other daytime activities will make your home feel larger and more generous in spirit.

"Elegance in the bedroom," says Chicago designer Janet Schirn, "should derive from *function*. Anything that contributes to your physical well-being and eliminates storage problems is marvelous—and essential—in the bedroom."

VEIL A TABLE

Slipcover a bedside table in sheer white silk gauze, made floor-length. "The silk creates a lovely volume of air around the table,"

says New York designer Benjamin Noriega-Ortiz. "It looks beautiful on absolutely any table that has a good shape." Note that this is literally a slipcover, not a tablecloth; the top is cut precisely to fit by a slipcover maker (ask a fabric store or friend to recommend a workroom), and the sides fall straight, not in folds. Have the hems rolled, if possible, and keep the design simple.

Tip: To clean, wash with Woolite in cold water, and drip-dry.

THE ACCOMMODATING CORNER

Even in a small bedroom, try to create a private niche that welcomes you for midday activities—sipping coffee, opening mail, working on your laptop. Plant a small round table (no more than 36 inches wide) near the window, along with one upholstered side chair (two if there's room). Keep a lamp on the table. Flowers, too. Eat lunch here once in a while, with a book.

Tip: To keep the table uncluttered, consider buying a tabouret (an artist's compact supply cart on wheels, from large art-supply stores). Its multitude of compartments will organize your stamps, pens, and paper, and you can park the phone on top. Slide it under the table, or use it as a nightstand.

WAKE UP, MAKE UP

If you've always longed for a real dressing table but think you lack the space, try placing a long, narrow table, like a console or sofa table, right at the foot of your bed. A stool or small-boned chair can tuck under the table; your mirror can stand on it; and perfumes and such can be marshaled into pretty boxes or onto trays. Choose a lamp with a slender base that won't steal too much space; run the cord under the bed to keep it out of view.

> **Tip:** *Avoid accessories that look like they belong in a bathroom, like a lighted mirror in a plastic frame. Look for a mirror on a handsome stand.*

THE AMAZING ARMOIRE

A very large armoire can make a small bedroom look bigger. It sounds strange, but it's true—the deception works in two ways. First, when your eye takes in the armoire's grand scale, you subconsciously assume that the room around it must be larger, too. Second, by stashing away many of your belongings, the armoire de-clutters the room and thereby makes it airier.

Bedroom Furniture in Supporting Roles

A FLASH OF MIRROR

Barry Dixon, a Washington, DC, designer, gets extra mileage from bedroom armoires by looking for period pieces with doors mirrored on the outside. "The mirrors add depth by reflecting space," he says. Look for an armoire with legs, not a solid base, he adds: they make a massive piece look lighter on its feet.

Tip: Consider having the armoire custom-shelved to hold your television, office supplies, and out-of-season sweaters. (Ask the store or antique dealer to recommend an expert carpenter.)

A FLASH OF MIRROR II

Another Barry Dixon solution to undersize bedrooms: Buy an immense framed mirror and lean it against the wall. "It suggests a doorway to another room, as if you're really in a suite of rooms," he says. It also reflects light, a bonus in any space.

Look for a mirror with doorway dimensions: roughly 32 to 38 inches wide, 72 to 84 inches high. If a framer has one ready-made, it will cost less than a custom job. Even better,

look for a Victorian specimen in a junque shop. (That's how Dixon found his, with ornamentation on top, for $350.) A crusty frame and mottled glass will only enhance the impression of antiquity.

Though the mirror will lean, have a good carpenter bolt it to the wall for safety reasons.

HEIGHTEN A CONTRAST

Highlight an antique bedside table by furnishing it with a lean, ultramodern, Italian-style halogen lamp. (Try the Tizio or the Berenice, both at good lighting stores and favorites of many designers.) "Modern lighting creates such an unexpected contrast with antiques," says Noriega-Ortiz, "that you become more aware of both the antique and the light."

DOZENS OF DRAWERS

Apothecary chests, with their myriad little drawers, are Janet Schirn's favorite nightstands. Save the top for a lamp and the book you're reading; stash everything else inside. (You'll have to switch to pocket-size packs of tissues, but it's worth it.) "A nightstand that accommodates everything you need," says

Schirn, "is a real luxury." For an antique apothecary chest, find dealers who specialize in Asian furnishings; for reproductions, try major furniture stores or catalogs.

Tip: If you do your nails in bed, an apothecary chest will hold all the supplies. Protect the top from spills with a sheet of beveled glass.

NO VISIBLE SUPPORT

"Float" the nightstands next to your bed. Buy two beautiful trays of metal or wood (contemporary or antique) and mount them on L-shaped metal brackets affixed to the wall. Paint the bottom of the L-brackets to match the wall. The trays will appear to be cantilevered.

Tip: The floating effect vanishes if the bottoms of the L-brackets show. Have a friend hold the arrangement in place so you can get the height right.

RETHINK THE NIGHTSTAND

Some designers use a beautiful writing desk right by the bed, instead of a traditional nightstand. It gives you a civilized spot for bill paying and letter writing; it vanquishes the traditional nightstand (rarely chosen for good looks anyway); it keeps your papers and magazines right at hand when you're in bed; and, of course, the same lamp serves both desk and bed.

Bedroom Furniture in Supporting Roles

THE DECORATIVE SHELF

Try to avoid store-bought bookshelves in a bedroom; they tend to be all function and no form. Instead, try this Martha Stewart technique for hanging great-looking shelves:

Affix decorative brackets to the wall in pairs, so they can support three or more shelves. For an unexpected airiness, leave plenty of room so the shelves are "stacked" 18 inches apart. (The brackets can be simple wood supports from Home Depot or a lumberyard, or wrought-iron ones from a catalog or flea market.) Finally, wrap wooden shelves in linen, using a staple gun in back to hold the fabric—it's a much softer look than paint.

Tip: For a terrific visual file of Stewart's ideas,
all of them generous with how-to instructions, see her book
Decorating Details (*Clarkson Potter*).

A USEFUL VIGNETTE

Many bedrooms have two closets on one wall, creating an empty slice of wall in between. Create a tableau for that often-neglected space, starting with a handsome bureau (or a

vintage bookcase no taller than 5 feet). Hang two to six mirrors or pictures, stacked, above the furniture, aligning the top
of the artwork with the top of the neighboring door frames.
Keep flowers, family photos, and other *objets* on the bureau.
Place a small, handsome rug in front.

Now the closet doors serve as visual bookends for an
arrangement that's useful as well as beautiful.

A GRACEFUL DESK

"The bedroom should be a place of repose, where you put
work aside," says San Francisco designer Joan Malter
Osburn. "But that's not always practical—some people have
to work there, too." Her tips for making the dual-purpose
bedroom succeed:

- Buy a writing desk that's gracious enough for a bedroom, but make sure it has at least a couple of drawers
  so you're not faced with work when you awaken.

- Use filing carts or cabinets on casters that can be rolled
  away under the desk. (See catalogs like Hold
  Everything and Levenger, listed in Chapter 6, or check
  out a large art-supply store.)

- Keep only good-looking objects on the desktop: a lovely piece of pottery to hold pens, a decoupaged box to catch papers, fresh flowers that you replace each week.

ROOM WITH A VIEW

If you spend many hours working in the bedroom, try to position the desk so you can look out the window. If that's not possible, create an interior view by hanging an oversize mirror—nearly as wide as the desk, if possible—just above the work surface, facing you. Or lean it against the wall, making sure you have it bolted in place by a good carpenter. The mirror will magnify light; more important, it becomes a window in its own right.

CONCEAL A BEDROOM OFFICE

Here's another use for an antique armoire: camouflaging a small home office. Ask the dealer or an expert carpenter to transform the interior for work, suggests Joan Malter Osburn. (Don't be afraid to cut away a section of the back to make room for a bulky computer.) Make rough sketches and measure until you know where the printer, fax, and phone will go; create openings in the back where cords can snake out. Have an electrician put outlets behind the armoire; run a phone jack there as well.

Tip: For ergonomic reasons, make the top of the monitor screen level with your gaze, and install a tiltable keyboard tray, so you can tilt the keyboard slightly down in back. (One good tray is the Flex-Rest; call [800] 336-7484 for information.)

THE WILD THINGS

Every room can borrow an exotic note from animal prints, and the bedroom is no exception. When upholstering or slip-covering a chair, chaise, or the ottoman at a dressing table, New York designer Craig Raywood prefers zebra-patterned fabric to the expected chintz. "Anything that comes from nature is a neutral, including animal prints," he says. "They don't have to match anything else in the room."

If there's nothing to slipcover, try a smaller accent: a zebra throw pillow for the bed; leopard-spotted wallpaper border under the crown molding; a 15-inch-tall band of tiger-stripe fabric along the bottom of plain white draperies.

THE EXPANSIVE SHELF

Books can transform a bedroom: they not only reflect your tastes but turn the space into a reading retreat. For a richer look than store-bought bookshelves offer, consider a custom-made, wall-to-wall shelving unit. Have it built on the window wall, always a good place for architectural cabinetry. Make it roughly 11 inches deep and just high enough to look like an extended windowsill. On a 13-foot-long wall, such a unit would give you 26 linear feet of shelving *plus* 13 feet of display space along the top.

If the shelving must enclose a radiator, make sure the carpenter gives you easy access (via hinged grilles). Have openings cut for access to electrical outlets, too. If a lamp will stand on the top ledge, a round hole cut nearby will let the cord "disappear" behind the books on the shelves below.

DREAM OF A DRESSING ROOM

Built-in shelving can also transform closets, making them inviting adjuncts to the bedroom. For terrific results, get sample plans and (free) estimates from at least two closet consultants; these people have storage solutions that are hard to come up with on your own. Done right, a professionally

Bedroom Furniture in Supporting Roles

81

organized closet will double, if not triple, your storage space without adding a single piece of freestanding furniture to the room. Add a few drawers to your built-in closet and you may even be able to eliminate a bureau from the bedroom.

HIGH TECH, HIGH TOUCH

If television-watching is part of your bedroom life, why hide it? Designer David Barrett came up with an exquisitely styl-

ish way of flaunting the TV in his own New York bedroom: He set it on a hand-carved tribal African table, with a tribal stool nearby to hold the VCR and cable box. The contrast of high-tech electronics with handmade or antique furniture comes off to the advantage of each.

> *Tip: It helps that the television, by Bang & Olufsen, has its own brand of elegance. The match of new and old works best when the "new" has a modern edge.*

Telling Details and Elegant Display

Just as a little Chanel bag puts the finishing polish on an outfit, the accessories in your bedroom—lamps, switchplates, pictures, pillows, flowers, and the objects you collect—telegraph your personal style.

Because these details are small they can easily break with tradition, and that alone makes them more expressive than the largest pieces of furniture. A mirrored switchplate evokes diamonds and glamour; a Roseville art-pottery vase implies a discerning eye and a romantic nature. Think of these things as your signature, or, as New York designer and author Alexandra Stoddard puts it, the "grace notes" of your design scheme. Indeed, at their most personal, these well-chosen details are tiny revelations to those who see them.

Certain accents will enhance virtually any bedroom, making it more resonant. For instance, even the smallest stroke of black, whether new or antique, adds instant depth and sophistication. White makes a crisp, fresh accent color (whether or not the walls are also white)—in picture mats, porcelains, silk lampshades, clock faces, Battenberg lace pillows. And Nan Lee, partner in the New York design and architecture firm Lee/Wimpenny, always brings in a shiny or reflective surface, like a mirror or metallic sheers. "They act like windows, adding another dimension," she says.

Finally, consider the ultimate $20 upgrade: an armload of fresh flowers (or just tall greens, if you're on a budget). They can instantly propel your bedroom into a state of grace.

LUXE UNDERFOOT

Give yourself the small luxury of a bedside rug—made from an old fur coat. The feeling of fur on bare feet is exquisite, and your conscience will be clear if you recycle an old fur and don't replace it with a new one. Most coats will yield a rug at least 2 by 3 feet, the smallest size for a bedside rug.

Tip: An upholsterer should have the equipment needed to stitch through fur; don't try it on a standard machine. A rug pad, easily cut to size, will keep your rug from slipping.

THE COLOR OF SUNRISE

For instant romance, change the bulbs in one or two bedroom lamps to a soft, dawnlike pink. This is old advice that many designers still honor, and the subtlety may surprise you. "These bulbs turn white walls ivory, not pink," says Chicago designer Janet Schirn. "On colored walls, they just cast a warm glow." Her personal choice: pink bulbs by Sylvania.

A ROOM OF MANY MOODS

If you read in bed, make the lamp at your bedside flexible so it can accommodate both high-wattage reading and low-

wattage romance. Have the lamp rewired—a minor procedure at a lighting store—so it can accommodate a three-way bulb of up to 150 watts. "The usual 60-watt bulb is insufficient for reading," says San Francisco designer Joan Malter Osburn, "and your needs change through the day."

CREATE A FAMILY GALLERY

Most designers feel that bedrooms, being private, are the best place to display personal photos. But what turns a handful of photographs into a stunning collection? The way they're treated. Have your best black-and-white family photos custom-matted in 8x10 or 11x14 mats to set them off like jewels. To save money, slip the mats into store-bought, not custom, frames. Hang the largest frames near the center of a grouping, or above a tabletop on which smaller photographs are clustered.

Tip: Save color photos, particularly those that look posed, for tabletop or bureau-top displays. Black-and-white pictures look more ancestral, or at least more artistic, and deserve the more prominent spots.

PICTURES FROM THE PAST

Old family photos bring so much intimacy and personal history to a bedroom that Kim DePole, a New York designer, advises clients to fake the effect. Almost any photo shop, she points out, can reprint your new color pictures (from prints or negatives) in sepia. Mat and frame them as lovingly as you would an ancestor's photo. The result: an instant sense of the past.

Tip: Avoid sepia photos in which people
appear with computers
or other modern items.

A GLEAM BY THE BED

Top a bureau, a nightstand, or a skirted table with mirror, which adds sparkle, or with glass, so you can make a collage underneath. (Try yellowing letters from flea market scrapbooks, ticket stubs from the opera, or friends' wedding invitations.)

Mirror can usually be as thin as a quarter of an inch; glass should be thicker. (The glass supplier will suggest a thickness that suits the dimensions of the piece.) Check prices from several suppliers; they vary surprisingly.

> *Tip: Always, always have glass and mirror beveled.*
> *This makes it look more expensive than it is*
> *and reveals a knowing attention to detail.*

MAKE THE LIGHT SHIMMER

Bright, reflective objects raise the wattage of a room by magnifying light, even in small quantities. Not only does this make decorating sense—it's also a tenet of feng shui, the ancient Chinese way to harmonious design. Colored-glass bottles, sheer metallic bronze curtains, and the gold-decorated Limoges dishes you inherited from your grandmother all qualify as bright.

"All these things sparkle and glitter and enhance the level of *chi*," or energy, writes Gina Lazenby in her beautifully photographed *Feng Shui House Book* (Watson-Guptill). "They are especially useful in dark corners and plain, undecorated areas."

CONCERTO FOR A BEDROOM

Decorate for all of your senses. Burn a scented votive candle (if it's away from fabrics and all things flammable). Smuggle the fresh flowers from your dining table to your nightstand. And remember the importance of sound; whether soothing or stimulating, it can instantly improve your mood and give the bedroom greater dimension.

Make room for a small CD player, and consider not only music, but recordings of nature that sound like rain and surf, a sensual indulgence in the dark. In the morning, try books on cassette; you can probably get through a chapter a day just while exercising. Audiobooks can be rented from Books On Tape, (800) 626-3333, or borrowed from the library.

Tip: Buy a wall-mounted CD organizer to keep the nightstands clear.

THE BREEZE OF A SUMMER PORCH

A ceiling fan harks back to more leisurely times. It also cools the room inexpensively, and there is something sensual about its air currents that an air conditioner can't provide.

Buy the simplest ceiling fan you can find (fancy ones look

like bad reproductions), and mount it on the longest stem you can safely install, as a fan hung low provides a stronger breeze. Don't install lighting on the fan; the fixtures rarely look good, and from that high, central position, they cast depressing shadows. Rely on lamps, sconces, or torchères instead.

Look at restored vintage fans, too; they are surprisingly beautiful. Two sources with modest catalogs are The Fan Man in Dallas, (214) 826-7700, and (no relation) The Fan Man in Oklahoma City, (405) 751-0933.

REPLACE DOORS WITH DRAPERIES

Examine the door to the bedroom closet. Has it aged badly, with trim lumpy from decades of repainting? If you can't afford to replace it with a handsome solid (not hollow) door and brass hinges, take it down altogether and install a curtain instead. Some suggestions:

- Avoid strong color contrasts between the walls and the curtain. With similar colors, the curtain becomes an architectural element.

- Make the curtain two and a half times as wide as the doorway opening, hem it across the top, and slide it over a tension rod. Install a tieback at one side to hold it out of your way. (Yes, it will slightly narrow the closet opening.)

- Give the curtain body. Have it lined if the fabric is

lightweight, and make sure you buy a fabric of visible quality.

- Make sure the closet is well lighted, preferably from the inside. Because a curtain can't be opened as fully as a door, it may cast a partial shadow on your clothes.

- Keep the old door in storage so it can be patched up and reinstalled if you move out.

TEMPLES TO MEMORY

In a private corner of your bedroom, create a personal shrine—a little altar that invites reflection on something important to you. Donna Sapolin, a magazine editor, keeps a small stone from every place she's visited or lived; for her, each stone on the tabletop or windowsill looks distinct from the others and embodies a private memory.

Jean McMann's *Altars and Icons* (Chronicle Books) reveals altars of striking simplicity. One woman keeps photos of her late mother on a bedroom windowsill, along with a porcelain cat and a tiny blue vase for fresh flowers. McMann found shrines on mantels, in niches, even on top of a personal computer—where you can always place a scented candle, a small

Telling Details and Elegant Display

framed picture, and perhaps a little carved box you've owned since childhood.

"A material thing—a stone, a photograph, an old shoe—can become a shrine when it is displayed in a way that evokes inspiration, memory, respect, or reverence," McMann writes. The bedroom, a true retreat, is an ideal home for so personal a display.

PORCELAIN ARTWORK

A surprising number of decorators bring dishes into the bedroom—not for dining but for display over the bed. The trick is to have a broad mix of plates and platters that are largely different, but that all adhere faithfully to a narrow theme (like majolica, or blue-and-white transferware, or vintage white ceramics).

A good arangement is roughly as wide as the bed and highest toward the center, as in a circle or triangle shape. To get it right, put a plate hanger (from any hardware store) on each plate. Trace the outer rim of the plate on plain paper, make a mark where the nail should go (as determined by the plate hanger), and cut it out. Move these "paper plates" around on the wall, using tape, until the arrangement pleases you. Drive the nails through the marks, rip down the

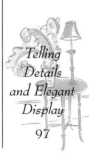

paper, and hang the plates: they'll be precisely where you want them.

PORCELAIN ARTWORK II

Another way to display porcelains in the bedroom is to run a long row of them just under the crown molding—or in lieu of crown molding, if you have none. Before hammering nails, tape up paper plates to get the intervals right. Start your arrangement over the room's major windows; try one or two plates over each, and take it from there.

If the plates are varied sizes, alternate them—inserting a dinner plate, for example, between every pair of smaller plates.

Tip: The china on your walls should look like a collection that's accrued over time. If you rush to fill in the gaps, your haste may show. Feel free to leave one or two walls undecorated until the right specimens turn up.

PAPER MOONS

As a romantic antidote to overhead bulbs in his upstate New York bedroom, artist Frank Faulkner made shades from white paper umbrellas. The glow of light through waxy white paper is almost moonlike, and the umbrella has a lovely, evocative shape.

Some careful work at the top of a ladder is required, but here's how New York lighting designer Ann Kale made her own paper-umbrella shades:

Remove the cover of your ceiling fixture. Replace the screws in the socket with screws half an inch longer, so they jut out. Buy a paper umbrella with a wood handle (try an import store), open it, and saw off the handle an inch below the spot where the spokes branch out. Weave wire through the spokes and around the jutting screws until the umbrella is held in place and has a nice tilt to it.

If you have access to a Chinese neighborhood, like New York's Chinatown, paper umbrellas run about $10 apiece. Or try Pearl River Mart's website, www.pearlriver.com; you'll need to custom-order by e-mail. Ask for either the 32-inch or 40-inch paper umbrella in white; both are around $12.

Tip: Use low-wattage bulbs to avoid a fire hazard.
You're going for a glow, not true illumination.

MOODY BLUES

Upgrade that plastic container of hand lotion that's ubiquitous on so many nightstands. Buy a cobalt-blue glass bottle with a pump top, sold in many beauty supply stores, and—very patiently—pour into it a moisturizer that's not overly thick. (Do this over the sink, not over the bed). The dark blue glass makes a pretty accent in any color scheme.

FINE LINES OF BLACK

It's widely said that every room needs a touch of black. Bedrooms are no exception, but here the black accents require a certain delicacy. Try black lacquer boxes. Or a black jasperware bowl to hold your earrings. Or a bamboo cabinet, as bamboo's golden tones are enhanced by natural brown-black markings.

You might even go flower shopping, as Barbara Southerland, a designer in Greenville, NC, and New York, recommends, and bring home an armload of purple-black Queen of Night tulips. (A good florist can order Queen of Night parrot tulips, with ruffled petals, for an exotic look.) Place in a glass vase, which won't compete with these high-drama flowers.

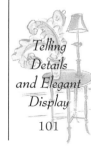

A GENEROUS LIGHT

What makes the perfect bedside lamp? One that's adjustable, clean-lined, and not greedy for space. Two classic possibilities:

- The Luxo, also known as an architect's lamp, has a form-follows-function brand of elegance. Buy it in white or stainless steel, advises designer Janet Schirn.

- The classic brass swing-arm light. Every lighting store carries these in a range of prices. Make sure yours moves easily on its hinges, and buy an electric-cord cover if you can't hide the wiring within the wall. A brass cord-cover will look good; so can plastic if you paint it to match the wall.

A HOSPITABLE LIGHT

Have an electrician wire your bedroom closet for overhead incandescent lighting. Better yet, add a motion sensor that turns the light on when you open the door, then turns it off some minutes later (even if you've left the closet door ajar). Being able to see your clothes clearly, says Joan Malter Osburn, is a bedroom necessity, not a luxury.

***Tip:** Paint the closet interior any light color that pleases you, says Osburn, and it will add sensory pleasure to your morning and evening routines.*

NEXT TO GODLINESS

Cleanliness matters everywhere, but most of all in this intimate room where you sleep, awaken, dress, lounge, make love. Hire a housekeeper, even if it's just a sporadic indulgence. Have the windows washed, the blinds or curtains professionally cleaned. Run an air purifier. Remember to clean the mirrors and scrub fingerprints off the door frames. Vacuum the moldings. Use natural citrus cleaners for their purity and scent (try the Harmony catalog, listed in Chapter 6). Cleanliness will make your bedroom even more of a daily sanctuary.

CULTIVATE BLOSSOMS

For inexpensive artwork that's worthy of framing for the bedroom, buy the softcover book *Flowers* by Haruhito Wako and Masato Kawai (Chronicle Books). Their extraordinary photographs are printed on cream-colored matte paper, and each

flower is so lovely you may need two copies of the book—to avoid having to choose between two sides of a page. Custom mats will make the square pages ready for store-bought frames in stock sizes, if you can't splurge on custom framing.

Tip: Ask the framer to slice the pages out of the book for you, to lower the risk of tearing.

KINDLE A SMALL FLAME

Scented candles are immeasureably romantic in a bed-room—a reminder to slow down, breathe deeply, and enjoy the day's smaller pleasures. Mimosa is a lovely scent; so are gardenia, lavender, tea rose, and fig. Experiment with different brands; some $34 candles will please you for weeks or months, but so will the occasional $3.99 bargain. Some candle wisdom:

- Choose candles with a light scent, not a strong one.

- Burn votive candles in heavy glass containers. *Don't* burn tapers; they tip more easily if bumped. Keep candles at a safe distance from bedroom hazards: sheets, curtains, the piles of paper on your writing desk. Do not leave unattended.

- Before lighting a candle, trim the wick to a quarter-inch. It will lengthen the candle's life. (So will keeping the flame out of breezes.)

- Light a candle as soon as you bring it home, if only for a moment. A candle with a virgin wick looks like a "decorator accessory."

CUT THE TETHER

For true liberation in the bedroom, buy a cordless telephone headset or a portable phone into which a headset can be plugged. You can now talk with both hands free, allowing you to put on makeup, dress, or make the bed while calling the office. (Try Radio Shack stores, or the Hello Direct catalog listed in Chapter 6.)

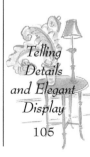

Telling Details and Elegant Display

THE ALLURE OF LITTLE BOXES

Banish bulky filing cabinets from a bedroom home office by keeping papers in handsome labeled boxes. Scott Salvador and Michael Zabriskie, a New York design team, keep financial papers and receipts in such boxes, stacked on built-in shelves in the bedroom. Letters, catalogs, cassette tapes, notebooks, office supplies, and photos can all be organized this way. Yes, the task of filing will demand a bit more work. But the boxes look so satisfyingly decorative that the extra effort is worth it.

Sources: Martha By Mail, Hold Everything, and Exposures Homes all sell sturdy and handsome storage boxes; these catalogs are listed in Chapter 6.

A LITTLE MORNING MUSIC

Hang a birdfeeder outside your bedroom window. The birdsong will attune you to nature early in the day.

CHAPTER ◆ 6

The Best Mail-Order Resources for Bedrooms

I've tried to include the quirky as well as the classic, particularly for readers who don't live near major shopping districts. Catalog prices do change, so they're not included here—but many of these catalogs are free.

Anthropologie
One Margaret Way
Ridgely, MD 21685
(800) 309-2500
www.anthropologie.com
    Vintage-looking bureau knobs, sheer draperies, a delicately scrolled iron bed reproduced by Amish ironworkers . . . a catalog as pleasingly quirky as the Anthropologie stores.

Ballard Designs
1670 DeFoor Avenue N.W.
Atlanta, GA 30318
(800) 367-2775

A rich mix of pieces that look fresh and antique at the same time: four-posters and bed drapery, Belgian linens, mosquito netting, fabric "slipcovers" for ceiling lighting fixtures; handsome lamps and clocks. Their low étagères with open shelving would make elegant night tables.

Banana Republic
5900 North Meadows Drive
Grove City, OH 43123
(888) 906-2800

Crisp bed linens, soft throws, decorative pillows in sweaterlike coverings. (Home furnishings are at the back of the catalog, after the clothes.)

Calico Corners
203 Gale Lane
Kennett Square, PA 19348
(800) 213-6366

Buying fabrics by mail may seem unwise, but these are clearly photographed; one-yard swatches can be borrowed, and the company's chain of stores is famous. Don't miss the great-looking furnishings, stuffed partially with goosedown and upholstered in your choice of material.

Charles P. Rogers Brass & Iron Beds
55 West 17th Street
New York, NY 10011
(800) 561-0467

Truly beautiful metal beds and the side tables to accompany them. A few styles, like the wrought-iron campaign bed, are so clean-lined they look almost modern. Close-up photos show the metal finishes, detailing, and joinery.

Crate & Barrel
P.O. Box 3200
Naperville, IL 60566
(800) 323-5461

All the basics, in clean-lined styles: beds and bedding, storage units for closets and bath, modern-looking desks and shelving that would not look out of place in a bedroom/home office.

Cuddledown of Maine
312 Canco Road
Portland, ME 04103
(800) 323-6793

Some intriguing finds among the sheets, towels, and beds: sheets with a 320-thread count, cowhide pillows stenciled with animal prints, and high-end sheets of pure silk and linen—so high-end they have to be air-dried. Check the website for clearance merchandise: www.cuddledown.com.

Design Toscano
1645 Greenleaf Avenue
Elk Grove Village, IL 60007
(800) 525-0733

This catalog is overrun with gargoyles but features a handful of cast ornaments that would look extraordinary in the bedroom, even over the bed: reproductions of eighteenth- and nineteenth-century relief sculptures that hang on the wall like friezes; a cast Gothic architectural detail; a miniature rose window to catch the sunlight.

Elements
P.O. Box 6105
Rapid City, SD 57709
(800) 778-5555
www.elementscatalogue.com

Bedding, rugs, standing screens, picture frames, leggy little tables, boxes, pillows—all in a lean, hip catalog from Spiegel.

The Best
Mail-Order
Resources
for
Bedrooms
109

Exposures Homes
P.O. Box 3615
Oshkosh, WI 54903
(800) 699-6993

Delicately painted furnishings, antique-white side tables, display shelves, and other pieces, plus candles, frames, and other pretty accessories.

Gardeners Eden
17 Riverside Street
Nashua, NH 03062
(800) 822-9600

Quite a few indoor furnishings, largely rustic in style: benches, chests, cabinets, lithe metal chairs, indoor fountains, even an armoire.

Garnet Hill
231 Main Street
Franconia, NH 03580
(800) 622-6216

Bedding of all kinds, from jersey knit sheets and pristine cotton to tempting cashmere throws. Also: beds, small tables (from metal to Moroccan), towels, vases, rugs, and other furnishings.

Harmony
360 Interlocken Boulevard, Suite 300
Broomfield, CO 80021
(800) 869-3446

Sheets, blankets, and other linens made of organic FoxFibre cotton and unbleached GreenCotton, mostly in shades of natural white and cream. Also: Zen rain chimes, a low-legged meditation table, and air filters (never a bad idea in the bedroom).

Hello Direct
5893 Rue Ferrari
San Jose, CA 95138
(800) 444-3556
   Many types of cordless phones and headsets.

Hold Everything
P.O. Box 7807
San Francisco, CA 94120
(800) 421-2264
   Good-looking accessories for organization, including storage supplies for closets, bedroom, and bath.

IKEA
8352 Honeygo Boulevard
Baltimore, MD 21236
(800) 434-IKEA
www.ikea.com
   Beds and bedding, rugs, drapery, picture frames, hooks, dressers, lamps, and towels. Stick to clean-lined pieces; they'll mix well with your better furnishings.

Illuminations
1995 South McDowell Boulevard
Petaluma, CA 94954
(800) CANDLES
   A wide and sensual assortment of candles, including the Rituals Candles formulated for such "essential qualities" as healing, abundance, and forgiveness.

J. Jill Homewear
P.O. Box 2006, 100 Birch Pond Drive
Tilton, NH 03276
(800) 642-9989
   The clothing company J. Jill now offers natural-looking bedding, towels, and

The Best Mail-Order Resources for Bedrooms

111

throws, in mixes of linen, hemp, washed velvet, chenille, and unbleached cotton. Interesting accents: seagrass lampshades; sheer organdy bed throws.

Kate's Paperie
561 Broadway
New York, NY 10012
Tel. (212) 941-9816
Fax (212) 941-9560

Decorative boxes; lamps with luminous paper shades; and large sheets of exotic handmade, even vegetable-dyed, papers that might cover the walls of a small niche. (Ask the store for advice before applying wallpaper paste.)

Legacy
514 North Third Street
Minneapolis, MN 55401
(800) 328-2711

Every three months Legacy comes out with a themed catalog—lodge style, for example, or Swedish style. In every genre, watch for beds and bedding, small tables, chairs, lamps, planters, mirrors, sconces, and storage pieces.

Lehman's Non-Electric Catalog
One Lehman Circle, P.O. Box 41
Kidron, OH 44636
(330) 857-5757
www.lehmans.com

This is the catalog from which the Amish order gas-powered refrigerators; it also offers pure beeswax candles, handmade soaps, and gorgeous Victorian metal brackets (called "bracket lamps") to hold pillar candles or small gas lamps. (Add the silvery glass reflector behind the bracket and magnify the light.)

Levenger
420 South Congress Avenue
Delray Beach, FL 33445
(800) 544-0880

Some great finds for the bedroom. Watch for elegant lamps, shelving, storage boxes, reading stands, writing desks.

Martha By Mail
P.O. Box 60060
Tampa, FL 33660
(800) 950-7130
www.marthastewart.com

Everything in this catalog comes in delicate hues, from pale blue to cloud gray to cream. My favorites from catalogs past: an oval, beveled mirror that hangs from a ribbon; sheer draperies with a two-foot-high linen hem, a silvered-glass lamp . . . the list goes on. Irresistible.

Mig and Tig Furniture
549 North Wells
Chicago, IL 60610
(312) 644-8277

Beds, including a "library bed" with shelves built into the headboard, and bedding, as well as bureaus, lighting, candles, and vases.

Mombasa
2345 Fort Worth Street
Grand Prairie, TX 75050
(800) 641-2345

A brochure-size catalog of mosquito nets—"woven from the threads of fantasy," as the company claims. Numerous styles, many colors. I'd stick to white.

The Best Mail-Order Resources for Bedrooms

113

Museum of Modern Art
Mail Order Department
11 West 53rd Street
New York, NY 10019
(800) 447-6662
www.moma.org

Modern classics. The Noguchi paper lamps cast a serene glow in a bedroom; also note the vases, candles and candlesticks, and lithe home-office furnishings.

Outwater Plastics Industries
4 Passaic Street, P.O. Drawer 403
Wood-Ridge, NJ 07075
(888) OUTWATER
www.outwater.com

This 929-page industrial catalog features products that may look strange at first, but wait: Amid the pipe fittings are plasterlike pilasters (flat columns) and other architectural ornaments, Victorian-looking wallcoverings, plaster busts of Apollo and David, cabinet hardware, and more. (Look toward the back.)

Pottery Barn
P.O. Box 7044
San Francisco, CA 94120
(800) 922-5507

Simple, classic pieces for bedrooms include beds, bedside tables, rugs, lighting, mirrors, candles, standing screens, and sheer draperies.

Restoration Hardware
104 Challenger Drive
Portland, TN 37148
(800) 762-1005

This company brings back old classics (1950s lighting, drawer pulls) and invents new ones (candles, clocks). It also sells Silver Sage paint, the exact shade of green used in the firm's stores—call for a swatch.

Room
151 West 30th Street, Suite 705
New York, NY 10001
(888) 420-ROOM

   Modern, but also comfortable, furnishings: beds and bedding, mirrors and lighting, and sensual accessories, like a bedside rug of woven leather. Room looks like a sleek design magazine, except that everything on its pages is for sale.

Shaker Workshops
P.O. Box 8001
Ashburnham, MA 01430
(800) 840-9121
www.shakerworkshops.com

   To buy assembled or in kits: Shaker-style beds, nightstands, candle stands, cupboards, armoires, handsome chests of drawers, oval boxes for storage, and a writing desk (billed as a worktable).

Sisal Rugs Direct
P.O. Box 313
Excelsior, MN 55331
(888) 613-1335
www.sisalrugs.com

   The Wall Street Journal ranked this as a top mail-order source for sisal rugs. There's more on the website than in the brochure-size catalog, and custom sizes and shapes are available.

Smith & Hawken Home & Clothing
2 Arbor Lane, Box 6900
Florence, KY 41022
(800) 776-3336
www.smith-hawken.com

   In one issue of this home furnishings catalog, the copy refers to "collaborations with nature," and that's what the products reflect. A picture frame is made of manzanita branches; a coffee table contains a recess where bulbs or grasses can grow.

The Best Mail-Order Resources for Bedrooms

Smith+Noble Windoware
P.O. Box 1838
Corona, CA 91718
(800) 248-8888

Fabric and bamboo shades, with linings for privacy, are perfectly suited to the bedroom; use them alone or behind draperies. Also: handsome wooden cornices, draperies in black velvet and white silk, and hardware. You measure and install, using the catalog's clear instructions.

Spiegel
P.O. Box 182555
Columbus, OH 43218
(800) 345-4500

Linens for the bed, plus the beds themselves. Also window treatments, lamps, rugs, mirrors, drapery, and hardware for curtains and bureau drawers. Look for magazine ads that discount the catalog price to about $6 from the usual $10.

Whispering Pines: Things for the Cabin
43 Ruane Street
Fairfield, CT 06430
(800) 836-4662

Rustic accessories for an Adirondacks hideaway: an old-fashioned sewing-box table; lamps with birch-log bases; quilts and bedding; picture frames well suited for bedside tables.